BLOOM
Founded by | arihant

Olympiad ACE

A Comprehensive Practice Book
for School Olympiads & Talent Search Exams

GENERAL KNOWLEDGE
Class 2

by
Suman Bharti

Olympiad ACE

BLOOM

Bloom Cap Edu Ventures Pvt. Ltd.

卐 **Administrative & Production Office**

'Ramchhaya' 4577/15, Agarwal Road, Darya Ganj, New Delhi -110002
Tele: 011- 47630600, 43518550

卐 **PRICE:** ₹125.00

Published by Arihant Publications (I) Ltd.

For further information about the books log on to
www.bloomcap.org

Follow us on

Preface

"Future belongs to those Who prepares for it today"

School Olympiads are National & International level competitions conducted by different Government, Non-Government & Educational Organisations with the purpose of making the children ready to face competitive exams. The challenging Questions asked in Olympiads motivate them to learn more & more and bring out the best result with improved academic performance. The Awards & Scholarship offered by Olympiads motivate children to aspire & strive for doing better and emerge out to be the best.

GK Olympiads

GK is the knowledge of every aspect of the human life, which may or may not be the part of routine academic studies but very important for the overall personality development of the students. It is more or less connected with the attentiveness and awareness. There can be different domains of GK like; History, Geography, Polity, Culture, Discovery, Sports, Current Affairs etc.

GK Olympiads help students in understanding the importance of General Knowledge and updations about National & International Affairs in daily life.

'Bloom GK Olympiad Study Book Class 2' is a perfect resource to Study & Practice for Olympiad Exams and other National & State Level Talent Search Exams & Other Competitions.

Some Special Features of Bloom GK Olympiad Study Books are;

- Complete coverage of all the topics related to GK;. History, Geography, Environment, Polity, Science, Sports, etc.
- Chapterwise Exercises having different types of Objective Questions.
- Olympiad Pattern Practice Sets at the end.

This book is prepared by Expert Panel with the utmost care, still if you have any suggestions regarding its improvement then feel free to contact us at support@bloomcap.org. We will try to inculcate your suggestions in the further editions.

Contents

01

Our Surroundings

1. **Which one of the following is mismatched?**
   (a) Hindu-Temple (b) Sikh-Gurudwara
   (c) Muslim-Church (d) Muslim-Mosque

2. **Which place is used to send and receive letters?**
   (a) Police station (b) Hospital
   (c) Fire station (d) Post office

3. **Who makes clays pots and diyas?**
   (a) Mechanic (b) Carpenter (c) Potter (d) Plumber

4. **Who sells medicines and bandages?**
   (a) Doctor (b) Nurse (c) Chemist (d) Fireman

5. **We go to which place when we are not well?**
   (a) Hospital (b) School (c) Police station (d) Park

6. **Who enforce rules and regulates movement of cars and bikes on roads?**
   (a) Traffic Policeman (b) Servant
   (c) Doctor (d) Postman

7. **At which of the following places we go to buy variety of things, which we need everyday?**
   (a) Police station (b) Market
   (c) Park (d) Restaurant

8. **Rahul's mother has one brother, Sohan. What is the relation of Sohan with Rahul?**
   (a) Cousin (b) Maternal uncle (c) Brother (d) Grandfather

9. **In which of the following places you will go to play with your friends?**
   (a) School (b) Park
   (c) Temple (d) Bank

10. **How policeman helps us?**

(a) Protects us from robbers and thieves
(b) Helps us in studies
(c) Collects garbage
(d) Sells fruits and vegetables

11. **Who protects us from enemy on the borders?**

(a) Plumber (b) Servant
(c) Doctor (d) Armyman

12. **Which one of the following you will find in hospital?**

(a) Doctor (b) Teacher
(c) Nurse (d) Both (a) and (c)

13. **Who makes railings and iron gates?**

(a) Tailor (b) Green grocers
(c) Blacksmith (d) Chemist

14. **In which of the following places we go to deposit our money and take it out when required?**

(a) Bank (b) School
(c) Doctor (d) Fire station

15. **The given equipment is used by which of the following?**

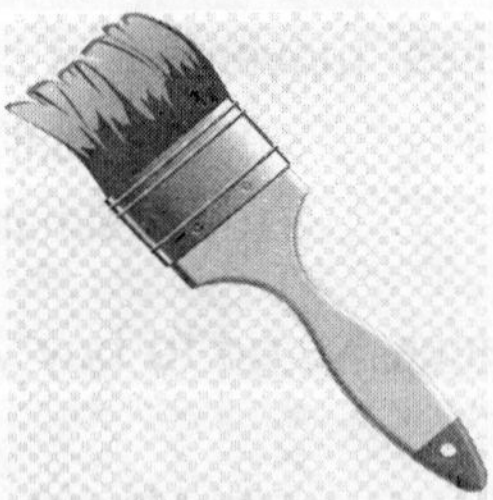

(a) Cobbler (b) Dentist
(c) Plumber (d) Painter

16. **What is my relation with my paternal uncle's father?**

(a) Grandson (b) Nephew (c) Cousin (d) Uncle

17. **Which one of the following you will not find in your school?**

(a) Teacher (b) Classmates (c) Principal (d) Farmer

18. **Sara's mother and Rubina's mother are sisters. Sara is Rubina's ....**

(a) Grand daughter (b) Aunt
(c) Cousin (d) None of these

19. **Which one of the following tasks is performed by carpenter?**

(a) He washes our clothes (b) He repairs our cars
(c) He repairs our furniture (d) He stitches our clothes

20. **It is the duty of the .... to take care of the patient and give proper treatment.**

(a) Tailor (b) Doctor (c) Cobbler (d) Postman

21. **If you go to a bakery shop near your house, what products you will get there?**

(a) Bread (b) Biscuits (c) Cakes (d) All of these

22. **Which one of the following tools is used by tailor?**

(a) Hammer (b) Nails (c) Scissors (d) Gun

23. **Match the following.**

List I (People)	List II (Work)
A. Tailor	1. Sells vegetables
B. Cobbler	2. Repairs automobiles
C. Mechanic	3. Mends shoes
D. Grocer	4. Stitches clothes

Codes

	A	B	C	D		A	B	C	D
(a)	4	3	2	1	(b)	3	4	1	2
(c)	2	3	4	1	(d)	1	2	3	4

Darken your choice with HB Pencil

1. ⓐ ⓑ ⓒ ⓓ	5. ⓐ ⓑ ⓒ ⓓ	9. ⓐ ⓑ ⓒ ⓓ	13. ⓐ ⓑ ⓒ ⓓ	17. ⓐ ⓑ ⓒ ⓓ	21. ⓐ ⓑ ⓒ ⓓ
2. ⓐ ⓑ ⓒ ⓓ	6. ⓐ ⓑ ⓒ ⓓ	10. ⓐ ⓑ ⓒ ⓓ	14. ⓐ ⓑ ⓒ ⓓ	18. ⓐ ⓑ ⓒ ⓓ	22. ⓐ ⓑ ⓒ ⓓ
3. ⓐ ⓑ ⓒ ⓓ	7. ⓐ ⓑ ⓒ ⓓ	11. ⓐ ⓑ ⓒ ⓓ	15. ⓐ ⓑ ⓒ ⓓ	19. ⓐ ⓑ ⓒ ⓓ	23. ⓐ ⓑ ⓒ ⓓ
4. ⓐ ⓑ ⓒ ⓓ	8. ⓐ ⓑ ⓒ ⓓ	12. ⓐ ⓑ ⓒ ⓓ	16. ⓐ ⓑ ⓒ ⓓ	20. ⓐ ⓑ ⓒ ⓓ	

02

Solar System

1. **Which is the 8th planet of our Solar System?**
(a) Jupiter (b) Neptune (c) Mars (d) Earth

2. **Which one of the following planets is the outer planet of our Solar System?**
(a) Venus (b) Uranus (c) Mercury (d) Mars

3. **Which one of the following planets is known as Evening/Morning Star?**
(a) Earth (b) Saturn (c) Venus (d) Jupiter

4. **What is the main feature of planet Jupiter?**
(a) It is the smallest planet (b) It is the biggest planet
(c) It is not a planet (d) None of these

5. **The smallest planet of our Solar System is ....**
(a) Mercury (b) Venus (c) Earth (d) Mars

6. **Which one of the following planets is known as Red Planet?**
(a) Jupiter (b) Saturn (c) Mercury (d) Mars

7. **Which of the following planets are considered as Twin's ?**
(a) Mercury and Venus (b) Venus and Earth
(c) Earth and Mars (d) Mars and Jupiter

8. **The path of each planet around the Sun is known as ....**
(a) orbit (b) axis
(c) revolve (d) None of these

9. **Which one of the following planets is closest to the Sun?**
(a) Mars (b) Jupiter (c) Saturn (d) Mercury

10. **The instrument which is used to see the planets is ....**
(a) telescope (b) microscope (c) kaleidoscope (d) camera

11. **Which planet of the Solar System is surrounded by ring-like structures?**
(a) Mercury (b) Mars (c) Earth (d) Saturn

12. **Our Solar System includes ....**
(a) Sun (b) planets (c) Moon (d) All of these

13. **Identify the planet that is located between Mars and Saturn.**
(a) Jupiter (b) Mercury (c) Earth (d) Uranus

14. **The movement of 365 days of the Earth around the Sun is known as ....**
(a) rotation (b) revolution
(c) orbit (d) axis

15. **Which of the following is not a planet?**
(a) Mars (b) Saturn (c) Moon (d) Venus

16. **Which planet is closest to the Sun?**
(a) Venus (b) Mercury (c) Earth (d) None of these

17. **The second largest planet of the Solar System is ....**
(a) Saturn (b) Jupiter (c) Uranus (d) Mars

18. **......... is the farthest planet from the Sun.**
(a) Saturn (b) Neptune
(c) Uranus (d) None of these

19. **Which among the following is known as the Red Planet in our Solar System?**
(a) Mars (b) Uranus
(c) Venus (d) Neptune

20. **The planets in Solar System do not give off light of their even. They reflect from the ....**
(a) Moon (b) Sun (c) Earth (d) other planets

21. **Life is found on how many planets of Solar System?**
(a) One (b) Two (c) Five (d) Six

22. **Due to which movement of the Earth, there is change of seasons?**
(a) Rotation (b) Revolution
(c) Spin (d) All of these

23. **Which of the following heavenly body has its own light?**
(a) Earth (b) Jupiter (c) Sun (d) Moon

24. Match the following.

List I	List II
A. 	1. New Moon
B. 	2. Crescent Moon
C. 	3. Full Moon

Codes

	A	B	C		A	B	C
(a)	1	2	3	(b)	1	3	2
(c)	2	3	1	(d)	2	1	3

Darken your choice with HB Pencil

1.	ⓐ ⓑ ⓒ ⓓ	5.	ⓐ ⓑ ⓒ ⓓ	9.	ⓐ ⓑ ⓒ ⓓ	13.	ⓐ ⓑ ⓒ ⓓ	17.	ⓐ ⓑ ⓒ ⓓ	21.	ⓐ ⓑ ⓒ ⓓ
2.	ⓐ ⓑ ⓒ ⓓ	6.	ⓐ ⓑ ⓒ ⓓ	10.	ⓐ ⓑ ⓒ ⓓ	14.	ⓐ ⓑ ⓒ ⓓ	18.	ⓐ ⓑ ⓒ ⓓ	22.	ⓐ ⓑ ⓒ ⓓ
3.	ⓐ ⓑ ⓒ ⓓ	7.	ⓐ ⓑ ⓒ ⓓ	11.	ⓐ ⓑ ⓒ ⓓ	15.	ⓐ ⓑ ⓒ ⓓ	19.	ⓐ ⓑ ⓒ ⓓ	23.	ⓐ ⓑ ⓒ ⓓ
4.	ⓐ ⓑ ⓒ ⓓ	8.	ⓐ ⓑ ⓒ ⓓ	12.	ⓐ ⓑ ⓒ ⓓ	16.	ⓐ ⓑ ⓒ ⓓ	20.	ⓐ ⓑ ⓒ ⓓ	24.	ⓐ ⓑ ⓒ ⓓ

03

My Country

1. **What is the National Anthem of our country?**
(a) Vande Mataram
(b) Jana Gana Mana
(c) Sare Jahan Se Accha
(d) None of these

2. **Which one of the following is the smallest state of India?**
(a) Rajasthan
(b) Goa
(c) Gujarat
(d) Punjab

3. **Which of the following states is located in the Southern part of India?**
(a) Punjab
(b) Haryana
(c) Himachal Pradesh
(d) Andhra Pradesh

4. **How many states are present in India?**
(a) 19
(b) 28
(c) 30
(d) 22

5. **Chandigarh is the capital of which state?**
(a) Rajasthan
(b) Delhi
(c) Punjab
(d) Uttar Pradesh

6. **What is the capital of India?**
(a) Bhopal
(b) Delhi
(c) Uttar Pradesh
(d) Maharashtra

7. **The famous market Chandni Chowk is located in which city?**
(a) Jaipur
(b) Kolkata
(c) Delhi
(d) Mumbai

8. **Find the odd one out.**
(a) Puducherry
(b) Chandigarh
(c) Lakshadweep
(d) Odisha

9. **What is the capital of Uttar Pradesh?**
(a) Lucknow
(b) Prayagraj
(c) Kanpur
(d) Agra

10. **Identify the Eastern most state of India.**
(a) Gujarat
(b) Arunachal Pradesh
(c) Odisha
(d) West Bengal

11. .... is popularly known for the production of tea.
(a) Himachal Pradesh (b) Telangana
(c) Karnataka (d) Assam

12. Which of the following cities of India is known as 'Space City of India'?
(a) New Delhi (b) Chennai
(c) Bengaluru (d) Mumbai

13. How many Union Territories are there in India?
(a) 6 (b) 7 (c) 8 (d) 9

14. What is the capital city of Madhya Pradesh?
(a) Bhopal (b) Jabalpur (c) Indore (d) Gwalior

15. The sequence of colour in our National Flag is ....
(a) saffron, white, green (b) white, saffron, green
(c) pink, white, green (d) green, blue, saffron

16. The city Mumbai is also known as ....
(a) City of Dreams (b) Hollywood of India
(c) City of Palaces (d) Both (a) and (b)

17. The lion capital of Ashoka is our ....
(a) National Anthem (b) National Emblem
(c) national song (d) national animal

18. Red Fort is situated in ....
(a) Mumbai (b) Rajasthan (c) Delhi (d) Tamil Nadu

19. Gateway of India is situated in ....
(a) Mumbai (b) Jammu and Kashmir
(c) Delhi (d) Kolkata

20. Which of the following Union Territories is also the capital of Haryana?
(a) Daman and Diu (b) Ladakh
(c) Delhi (d) Chandigarh

21. Which one of the following cities is the capital of Himachal Pradesh?
(a) Shimla (b) Kufri (c) Dharamshala (d) Mussoorie

22. The famous Marine Drive is located in which city?
(a) Kolkata (b) Bengaluru
(c) Chennai (d) Mumbai

23. Which state is known as Sugar Bowl of India?

(a) Gujarat (b) Rajasthan
(c) Uttar Pradesh (d) Madhya Pradesh

24. In which of the following states, the tallest statue of India is located?

(a) Manipur (b) West Bengal
(c) Odisha (d) Gujarat

25. Find the mismatched pair.

	State	Capital
(a)	Uttar Pradesh	Lucknow
(b)	Tamil Nadu	Chennai
(c)	Maharashtra	Nagpur
(d)	Uttarakhand	Dehradun

Darken your choice with HB Pencil

1.	ⓐ ⓑ ⓒ ⓓ	6.	ⓐ ⓑ ⓒ ⓓ	11.	ⓐ ⓑ ⓒ ⓓ	16.	ⓐ ⓑ ⓒ ⓓ	21.	ⓐ ⓑ ⓒ ⓓ
2.	ⓐ ⓑ ⓒ ⓓ	7.	ⓐ ⓑ ⓒ ⓓ	12.	ⓐ ⓑ ⓒ ⓓ	17.	ⓐ ⓑ ⓒ ⓓ	22.	ⓐ ⓑ ⓒ ⓓ
3.	ⓐ ⓑ ⓒ ⓓ	8.	ⓐ ⓑ ⓒ ⓓ	13.	ⓐ ⓑ ⓒ ⓓ	18.	ⓐ ⓑ ⓒ ⓓ	23.	ⓐ ⓑ ⓒ ⓓ
4.	ⓐ ⓑ ⓒ ⓓ	9.	ⓐ ⓑ ⓒ ⓓ	14.	ⓐ ⓑ ⓒ ⓓ	19.	ⓐ ⓑ ⓒ ⓓ	24.	ⓐ ⓑ ⓒ ⓓ
5.	ⓐ ⓑ ⓒ ⓓ	10.	ⓐ ⓑ ⓒ ⓓ	15.	ⓐ ⓑ ⓒ ⓓ	20.	ⓐ ⓑ ⓒ ⓓ	25.	ⓐ ⓑ ⓒ ⓓ

04

Our President, PMs and CMs

1. **Who was the first Prime Minister of India?**
(a) Mahatma Gandhi
(b) Sardar Vallabhbhai Patel
(c) Subhash Chandra Bose
(d) Jawaharlal Nehru

2. **Indira Gandhi was the .... woman Prime Minister of India.**
(a) first
(b) second
(c) third
(d) fourth

3. **Which of the following former Presidents was also a scientist?**
(a) Ram Nath Kovind
(b) Pranab Mukherjee
(c) Pratibha Patil
(d) APJ Abdul Kalam

4. **Who was the first woman President of India?**
(a) Indira Gandhi
(b) Sarojini Naidu
(c) Annie Besant
(d) Pratibha Patil

5. **Dr Rajendra Prasad was elected as first .... of India.**
(a) Prime Minister
(b) Chief Minister
(c) President
(d) Both (a) and (c)

6. **Which of the following Prime Ministers gave the slogan 'Jai Jawan Jai Kisan'?**
(a) Jawaharlal Nehru
(b) Indira Gandhi
(c) Lal Bahadur Shastri
(d) Narendra Modi

7. **Who is the Prime Minister of India?**
(a) Manmohan Singh
(b) Narendra Modi
(c) Pranab Mukherjee
(d) Yogi Adityanath

8. **Who was the first Vice-President of India?**
(a) Rajendra Prasad
(b) APJ Abdul Kalam
(c) Sarvepalli Radhakrishnan
(d) Sardar Patel

9. **Yogi Adityanath is the Chief Minister of which state?**

(a) Uttar Pradesh (b) Madhya Pradesh
(c) Rajasthan (d) Gujarat

10. **Identify the personality shown in the given picture.**

(a) Smriti Irani (b) Pratibha Patil
(c) Mamata Banerjee (d) Nirmala Sitaraman

11. **Identify the personality shown in the given picture.**

(a) Manmohan Singh (b) Rajnath Singh
(c) Sanjay Gandhi (d) Charan Singh

12. **Identify the personality shown in the given picture.**

(a) Narendra Modi (b) Atal Bihari Vajpayee
(c) Lal Bahadur Shastri (d) Sardar Patel

13. Who among the following Prime Ministers had served for the longest term?

(a) Jawaharlal Nehru (b) Atal Bihari Vajpayee
(c) Manmohan Singh (d) Narendra Modi

15. Identify the personality shown in the given picture.

(a) Yogi Adityanath (b) Arvind Kejriwal
(c) Amit Shah (d) Uddhav Thackeray

16. Who is the President of India?

(a) Droupadi Murmu (b) Pranab Mukherjee
(c) Ram Nath Kovind (d) None of these

17. Jagdeep Dhankar is the current .... of India.

(a) President (b) Vice-President (c) Prime Minister (d) None of these

18. 'Garibi Hatao' was the slogan given by ....

(a) Jawaharlal Nehru (b) Indira Gandhi
(c) Lal Bahadur Shastri (d) Narendra Modi

Darken your choice with HB Pencil

1.	ⓐ ⓑ ⓒ ⓓ	4.	ⓐ ⓑ ⓒ ⓓ	7.	ⓐ ⓑ ⓒ ⓓ	10.	ⓐ ⓑ ⓒ ⓓ	13.	ⓐ ⓑ ⓒ ⓓ	16.	ⓐ ⓑ ⓒ ⓓ
2.	ⓐ ⓑ ⓒ ⓓ	5.	ⓐ ⓑ ⓒ ⓓ	8.	ⓐ ⓑ ⓒ ⓓ	11.	ⓐ ⓑ ⓒ ⓓ	14.	ⓐ ⓑ ⓒ ⓓ	17.	ⓐ ⓑ ⓒ ⓓ
3.	ⓐ ⓑ ⓒ ⓓ	6.	ⓐ ⓑ ⓒ ⓓ	9.	ⓐ ⓑ ⓒ ⓓ	12.	ⓐ ⓑ ⓒ ⓓ	15.	ⓐ ⓑ ⓒ ⓓ	18.	ⓐ ⓑ ⓒ ⓓ

05

Country, Capital and Flag

1. **India's flag is known as ....**

(a) Tiranga (b) Union Jack
(c) Maple Leaf Flag (d) Lal Sobuj

2. **The given flag belongs to which of the following countries?**

(a) United States of America (b) Canada
(c) France (d) United Kingdom

3. **The flag shown in the image belongs to which country?**

Hint : Its capital is Canberra

(a) Japan (b) China (c) Thailand (d) Australia

4. **Which one of the following is the capital of Japan?**

(a) Tokyo (b) London (c) Paris (d) Dhaka

5. **What is the capital of Afghanistan?**

(a) Abu Dhabi (b) Kabul (c) Dhaka (d) Beijing

6. **Which one of the following is the capital of Canada?**

(a) Beijing (b) Ottawa (c) Paris (d) Colombo

7. **Beijing is the capital of ....**
(a) Bangladesh (b) Bhutan (c) China (d) Nepal

8. **Identify the country from the flag given below.**

(a) USA (b) United Kingdom
(c) Australia (d) Israel

9. **Dhaka is the capital of ....**
(a) Sri Lanka (b) China (c) Bangladesh (d) Egypt

10. **Identify the country from the given flag.**

(a) Bangladesh (b) Sri Lanka (c) Australia (d) Pakistan

11. **The given flag in the picture is representing, which of the following countries?**

(a) China (b) Japan (c) Bangladesh (d) France

12. What is the capital of Russia?

(a) Tokyo (b) Madrid (c) Rome (d) Moscow

13. Which one of the following is the capital of Italy?

(a) Colombo (b) Islamabad (c) Rome (d) Berlin

14. The given flag is the National Flag of which of the following countries?

(a) USA (b) UK (c) Australia (d) China

15. Which one of the following is the capital of France?

(a) Beijing (b) London (c) Paris (d) Manila

16. The statue shown in the picture is in which country?

(a) USA (b) Germany

(c) Russia (d) Australia

Darken your choice with HB Pencil

1.	ⓐ ⓑ ⓒ ⓓ	4.	ⓐ ⓑ ⓒ ⓓ	7.	ⓐ ⓑ ⓒ ⓓ	10.	ⓐ ⓑ ⓒ ⓓ	13.	ⓐ ⓑ ⓒ ⓓ	16.	ⓐ ⓑ ⓒ ⓓ
2.	ⓐ ⓑ ⓒ ⓓ	5.	ⓐ ⓑ ⓒ ⓓ	8.	ⓐ ⓑ ⓒ ⓓ	11.	ⓐ ⓑ ⓒ ⓓ	14.	ⓐ ⓑ ⓒ ⓓ		
3.	ⓐ ⓑ ⓒ ⓓ	6.	ⓐ ⓑ ⓒ ⓓ	9.	ⓐ ⓑ ⓒ ⓓ	12.	ⓐ ⓑ ⓒ ⓓ	15.	ⓐ ⓑ ⓒ ⓓ		

06

Fairs, Festivals and Religion

1. .... is the harvest festival celebrated in Kerala.
(a) Onam (b) Hornbill (c) Bihu (d) Pongal

2. Pongal is celebrated in which of the following states?
(a) Punjab (b) Odisha
(c) Madhya Pradesh (d) Tamil Nadu

3. Which one of the following is not a national festival of India?
(a) Independence Day (b) Baisakhi
(c) Gandhi Jayanti (d) Republic Day

4. Which of the following is/are religious festival?
(a) Republic Day (b) Christmas
(c) Eid (d) Both (b) and (c)

5. Gudi Parwa and Ganesh Chaturthi are the famous festivals of which of the following states?
(a) Uttar Pradesh (b) Karnataka (c) Punjab (d) Maharashtra

6. Identify the festival that is celebrated in the state of Assam.
(a) Bihu (b) Baisakhi (c) Losar (d) Bundi

7. On which festival, we burn the effigies of Ravana, his brother and son?
(a) Holi (b) Dussehra (c) Eid (d) Christmas

8. Which of these is a place of worship?
(a) Mosque (b) Church (c) Gurudwara (d) All of these

9. .... fair is held in Rajasthan every year.
(a) Kumbh Mela (b) Pushkar Mela (c) Hornbill Mela (d) Craft Mela

10. **Name the festival which is celebrated as the birth of Jesus Christ.**
(a) Raksha Bandhan (b) Dusshera
(c) Christmas (d) Republic Day

11. **Quran is the holy book of which religion?**
(a) Christians (b) Muslims (c) Hindus (d) Parsis

12. **Which festival is celebrated by Muslims at the end of the fasting month of Ramadan?**
(a) Durga Puja (b) Eid (c) Good Friday (d) Diwali

13. **Which one of the following festivals is the symbol of love between brother and sister?**
(a) Dusshera (b) Holi
(c) Raksha Bandhan (d) Christmas

14. **......... is worshipped on the occasion of Janmashtami.**
(a) Lord Hanuman (b) Lord Ganesha
(c) Lord Ram (d) Lord Krishna

15. **Durga Puja is the main festival of which state?**
(a) Karnataka (b) West Bengal
(c) Punjab (d) Uttarakhand

16. **Which of these festivals is celebrated in Punjab?**
(a) Durga Puja (b) Dussehra (c) Lohri (d) Holi

17. **Which festival is celebrated as 'Victory of good over evil'?**
(a) Diwali (b) Dusshera (c) Holi (d) Christmas

18. **Which festival is celebrated as the birth of Lord Krishna?**
(a) Navratri (b) Diwali
(c) Janmashtami (d) Maha Shivratri

19. **The first Guru of Sikh community is ....**
(a) Guru Nanak (b) Guru Gobind Singh
(c) Guru Arjan Dev (d) Gurudev

20. **The Ramayana and the Mahabharata are the epic books of which religion?**
(a) Sikhism (b) Hinduism (c) Islam (d) Christianity

21. **Which one of the following is the holy book of the Christians?**

(a) Avesta
(b) Guru Granth Sahib
(c) Bible
(d) Bhagavad Gita

22. **What is the harvest festival of Punjab?**

(a) Lohri (b) Onam (c) Pongal (d) Makar Sankranti

23. **The Rath Yatra in Puri is the famous festival celebrated in which of the following states?**

(a) Jammu and Kashmir
(b) Karnataka
(c) West Bengal
(d) Odisha

24. **In which of the following states, Surajkund Mela, the world's largest International Crafts Fair held ?**

(a) Uttar Pradesh (b) Rajasthan (c) Haryana (d) Maharashtra

25. **During which national festival, Parades are held at India Gate?**

(a) Independence Day
(b) Republic Day
(c) Gandhi Jayanti
(d) None of these

26. **The Holi festival celebrated every year is considered as.......... .**

(a) festival of joy
(b) festival of colours
(c) festival of light
(d) festival of war

27. **Which one of the following is the holy place of Muslims?**

(a) Golden Temple
(b) Kedarnath Temple
(c) Mecca-Madina
(d) Shimla Christ Church

28. **Which one of the following Hindu Goddess is known as Goddess of learning, wisdom and music?**

(a) Maa Laxmi
(b) Maa Durga
(c) Maa Saraswati
(d) Maa Kali

Darken your choice with HB Pencil

1.	a b c d	6.	a b c d	11.	a b c d	16.	a b c d	21.	a b c d	26.	a b c d
2.	a b c d	7.	a b c d	12.	a b c d	17.	a b c d	22.	a b c d	27.	a b c d
3.	a b c d	8.	a b c d	13.	a b c d	18.	a b c d	23.	a b c d	28.	a b c d
4.	a b c d	9.	a b c d	14.	a b c d	19.	a b c d	24.	a b c d		
5.	a b c d	10.	a b c d	15.	a b c d	20.	a b c d	25.	a b c d		

07

Music and Dance

1. **Which of these musical instruments is played by using only fingers?**
   (a) Drum (b) Piano (c) Flute (d) Trumpet

2. **Garba and Dandiya Rass are the famous dance forms of which of the following states?**
   (a) Rajasthan (b) Uttar Pradesh (c) Karnataka (d) Gujarat

3. **Kathak is classical dance of ....**
   (a) Uttar Pradesh (b) Maharashtra
   (c) Kerala (d) Rajasthan

4. **The classical dance Kathakali belongs to which of the following states?**
   (a) Maharashtra (b) Rajasthan (c) Kerala (d) Madhya Pradesh

5. **How many notes of Sur are present in Hindustani music?**
   (a) 7 (b) 8 (c) 6 (d) 9

6. **Which of the following is/are the famous dance(s) of the state Punjab?**
   (a) Giddha (b) Bhangra (c) Lavani (d) Both (a) and (b)

7. **What is the name of the instrument usually depicted holding or playing by Goddess Saraswati?**
   (a) Guitar (b) Sitar (c) Violin (d) Veena

8. **Identify the given instruments.**

   (a) Tabla (b) Harmonium
   (c) Sitar (d) Flute

9. **AR Rahman is a famous ....**

(a) dancer (b) musician (c) actor (d) director

10. **Which dance form is performed as a part of the Navratri celebrations?**

(a) Giddha (b) Lavani
(c) Bhangra (d) Garba

11. **Identify the musical instrument.**

(a) Guitar (b) Violin (c) Flute (d) Sitar

12. **'Kuchipudi' is a ....**

(a) dance (b) musical instrument
(c) song (d) None of these

13. **The dance shown in the image is ....**

(a) Kuchipudi (b) Bhangra (c) Kathak (d) Bharatanatyam

14. **Identify the famous singer shown in the given picture.**

(a) Shaan (b) Armaan Malik
(c) Udit Narayan (d) Sonu Nigam

15. Which of these instruments does not have strings?

(a) Harmonium (b) Guitar

(c) Violin (d) Veena

16. Find the odd one out.

(a) Tabla (b) Bhangra (c) Veena (d) Violin

17. Which one of the following is not a musical instrument?

(a) Harmonium (b) Spanner

(c) Flute (d) Trumpet

18. Which one of the following instruments is played by famous Indian Musician Ustad Zakir Hussain?

(a) Flute (b) Guitar

(c) Tabla (d) Violin

19. Which one of the following is the famous dance form of the state Rajasthan?

(a) Ghoomar (b) Mohiniyattam

(c) Kathak (d) Kuchipudi

20. The famous dance form Manipuri is form of which state?

(a) Mizoram (b) Tripura

(c) Meghalaya (d) Manipur

21. What is the name of the famous musician who played 'Shehnai'?

(a) Ustad Bismillah Khan (b) Ustad Zakir Hussain

(c) Shiv Kumar Sharma (d) Arijit Singh

22. Find the odd one out.

(a) Kirtan (b) Qawwali

(c) Ghazal (d) Violin

Darken your choice with HB Pencil

1.	ⓐ ⓑ ⓒ ⓓ	**5.**	ⓐ ⓑ ⓒ ⓓ	**9.**	ⓐ ⓑ ⓒ ⓓ	**13.**	ⓐ ⓑ ⓒ ⓓ	**17.**	ⓐ ⓑ ⓒ ⓓ	**21.**	ⓐ ⓑ ⓒ ⓓ
2.	ⓐ ⓑ ⓒ ⓓ	**6.**	ⓐ ⓑ ⓒ ⓓ	**10.**	ⓐ ⓑ ⓒ ⓓ	**14.**	ⓐ ⓑ ⓒ ⓓ	**18.**	ⓐ ⓑ ⓒ ⓓ	**22.**	ⓐ ⓑ ⓒ ⓓ
3.	ⓐ ⓑ ⓒ ⓓ	**7.**	ⓐ ⓑ ⓒ ⓓ	**11.**	ⓐ ⓑ ⓒ ⓓ	**15.**	ⓐ ⓑ ⓒ ⓓ	**19.**	ⓐ ⓑ ⓒ ⓓ		
4.	ⓐ ⓑ ⓒ ⓓ	**8.**	ⓐ ⓑ ⓒ ⓓ	**12.**	ⓐ ⓑ ⓒ ⓓ	**16.**	ⓐ ⓑ ⓒ ⓓ	**20.**	ⓐ ⓑ ⓒ ⓓ		

08

Famous Places

1. **Which one of the following monuments will you not find in New Delhi?**
(a) Taj Mahal (b) Red Fort (c) Qutub Minar (d) Jantar Mantar

2. **The famous monument shown in the picture is ....**

(a) Lotus Temple (b) Akshardham Temple
(c) Golden Temple (d) Birla Temple

3. **Which of the following monuments is one of the wonders of the world?**
(a) India Gate (b) Lotus Temple
(c) Taj Mahal (d) Gateway of India

4. **In which of the following cities, The Gateway of India is located?**
(a) Delhi (b) Kolkata (c) Chennai (d) Mumbai

5. **Identify the given monument.**

(a) Char Minar (b) Lotus Temple
(c) Hawa Mahal (d) Gateway of India

6. **What is the name of the world's tallest statue located in Gujarat?**
(a) Mahatma Gandhi Statue (b) Statue of Freedom
(c) Statue of Liberty (d) Statue of Unity

7. **Which one of the following monuments is a tall tower?**
(a) Taj Mahal (b) India Gate
(c) Jantar Mantar (d) Qutub Minar

8. **Lotus Temple is situated in ....**
(a) Delhi (b) Jaipur (c) Lucknow (d) Patna

9. **Our Prime Minister hoists the flag on which of the monument on Independence Day?**
(a) Jantar Mantar (b) India Gate
(c) Red Fort (d) Akshardham Temple

10. **............... was built to pay tribute to the soldiers died in First World War.**
(a) India Gate (b) Qutub Minar (c) Char Minar (d) Taj Mahal

11. **Which temple is located in Amritsar, Punjab?**
(a) Lotus Temple (b) Birla Temple
(c) Akshardham Temple (d) Golden Temple

12. **Agra Fort is located in which state?**
(a) New Delhi (b) Rajasthan (c) Haryana (d) Uttar Pradesh

13. **The official residence of our President is known as............ .**
(a) Parliament (b) Taj Mahal
(c) Rashtrapati Bhawan (d) Lok Sabha

14. **In which of the following States/Union Territories, the famous 'Rock Garden' is located?**
(a) Telangana (b) Puducherry (c) Chandigarh (d) Punjab

15. **Identify the famous building shown in the given picture.**

(a) Rashtrapati Bhawan (b) Parliament
(c) India Gate (d) Delhi Gate

16. **............... is known as the City of Lakes.**

(a) Jaipur (b) Udaipur (c) Mumbai (d) Nagpur

17. **Which of the following places is famous as 'Heaven on Earth'?**

(a) Kashmir (b) Shimla (c) Mussoorie (d) Udaipur

18. **The famous Sun Temple is located in which city?**

(a) Konark (b) Sambalpur (c) Rourkela (d) Belgaum

19. **Which city is famous as Pink City?**

(a) Jaipur (b) Agra (c) Udaipur (d) Mathura

20. **In which of the following states the biggest cricket stadium is located?**

(a) Andhra Pradesh (b) Tamil Nadu

(c) Punjab (d) Gujarat

21. **The pilgrimages located in Uttarakhand is/are............ .**

(a) Haridwar (b) Kedarnath (c) Badrinath (d) All of these

22. **............... is built on the banks of River Yamuna.**

(a) Golden Temple (b) Akshardham Temple

(c) Taj Mahal (d) Buland Darwaza

23. **Shimla, Nainital, Mussoorie are famous ....**

(a) beaches (b) hill stations (c) monuments (d) cities

24. **The mosque 'Jama Masjid' is located in which of the following cities?**

(a) New Delhi (b) Haridwar (c) Mussoorie (d) Nainital

Darken your choice with HB Pencil

1.	ⓐ ⓑ ⓒ ⓓ	5.	ⓐ ⓑ ⓒ ⓓ	9.	ⓐ ⓑ ⓒ ⓓ	13.	ⓐ ⓑ ⓒ ⓓ	17.	ⓐ ⓑ ⓒ ⓓ	21.	ⓐ ⓑ ⓒ ⓓ
2.	ⓐ ⓑ ⓒ ⓓ	6.	ⓐ ⓑ ⓒ ⓓ	10.	ⓐ ⓑ ⓒ ⓓ	14.	ⓐ ⓑ ⓒ ⓓ	18.	ⓐ ⓑ ⓒ ⓓ	22.	ⓐ ⓑ ⓒ ⓓ
3.	ⓐ ⓑ ⓒ ⓓ	7.	ⓐ ⓑ ⓒ ⓓ	11.	ⓐ ⓑ ⓒ ⓓ	15.	ⓐ ⓑ ⓒ ⓓ	19.	ⓐ ⓑ ⓒ ⓓ	23.	ⓐ ⓑ ⓒ ⓓ
4.	ⓐ ⓑ ⓒ ⓓ	8.	ⓐ ⓑ ⓒ ⓓ	12.	ⓐ ⓑ ⓒ ⓓ	16.	ⓐ ⓑ ⓒ ⓓ	20.	ⓐ ⓑ ⓒ ⓓ	24.	ⓐ ⓑ ⓒ ⓓ

09

Human Body

1. **Which one of the following is not a part of hands?**
   (a) Knee (b) Arm
   (c) Wrist (d) Elbow

2. **............... protect us from external environment and germs.**
   (a) Tongue (b) Skin (c) Teeth (d) Eyes

3. **Which organ helps in breathing?**
   (a) Lungs (b) Heart
   (c) Stomach (d) Brain

4. **Every human being has one .... to taste different food items.**
   (a) hand (b) leg (c) eye (d) tongue

5. **Identify the body part that helps us to smell our favourite food.**
   (a) Nose (b) Ears
   (c) Eyes (d) Tongue

6. **We cannot see anything, without which sense organ?**
   (a) Ears (b) Brain (c) Eyes (d) Heart

7. **Name the organ that helps in blood circulation in the body.**
   (a) Lungs (b) Kidney
   (c) Nose (d) Heart

8. **The sense organ help that us to listen to our teachers is ....**
   (a) Ears (b) Eyes (c) Brain (d) Heart

9. **Which parts of body, regrow again when we cut it?**
   (a) Nails (b) Hairs
   (c) Fingers (d) Both (a) and (b)

10. Pick the odd one out

(a) 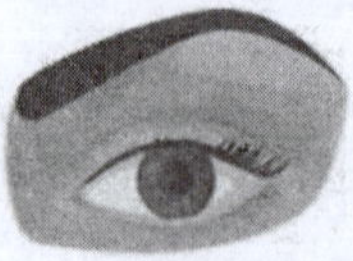

(b) 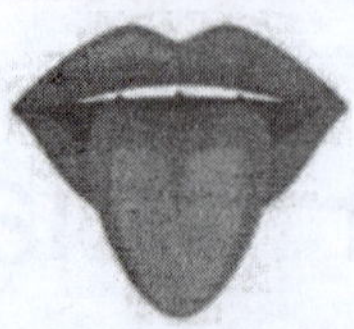

(c) 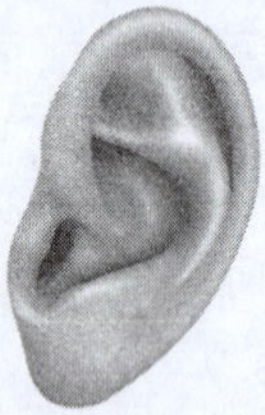

(d) 

11. Identify the organ which beats faster when we run.

(a) Brain (b) Heart (c) Legs (d) Eyes

12. .... helps us to think and to take decisions.

(a) Heart (b) Kidneys (c) Lungs (d) Brain

13. The organ which break the food into pieces in our mouth is ....

(a) tongue (b) teeth (c) nails (d) lips

14. Which part of the body helps us to lift, throw, push and pull?

(a) Legs (b) Heart (c) Arms (d) Knees

15. Which one of the following is a sense organ?

(a) Kidneys (b) Brain (c) Lungs (d) Skin

16. Which of the following body parts is called 'storehouse of knowledge'?

(a) Hands (b) Eyes (c) Brain (d) Nose

17. Which part of the body is not present in a pair?

(a) Lung (b) Kidney (c) Heart (d) Ear

18. The lungs are located inside which of the following parts?

(a) Legs (b) Brain (c) Mouth (d) Chest

19. What is the work done by stomach in our body?

(a) To provide oxygen (b) To circulate the blood

(c) To listen (d) To digest the food

20. Which of the following parts of human body is a memory keeper?

(a) Heart (b) Brain (c) Hands (d) Tongue

21. Which of the following is an internal organ?

(a) Kidneys (b) Palm (c) Nose (d) Chest

22. How many bones are there in human body?

(a) 206 (b) 310 (c) 115 (d) 76

23. Which one of the following is the soft part of our body?

(a) Teeth (b) Bones (c) Muscles (d) None of these

24. Match the following.

List I (Body Parts)	List II (Located At)
A. Nails	1. Hands
B. Ears	2. Legs
C. Foot	3. Head
D. Wrist	4. Fingers

Codes

	A	B	C	D		A	B	C	D
(a)	1	2	3	4	(b)	2	3	4	1
(c)	3	4	1	2	(d)	4	3	2	1

Darken your choice with HB Pencil

1.	ⓐ ⓑ ⓒ ⓓ	5.	ⓐ ⓑ ⓒ ⓓ	9.	ⓐ ⓑ ⓒ ⓓ	13.	ⓐ ⓑ ⓒ ⓓ	17.	ⓐ ⓑ ⓒ ⓓ	21.	ⓐ ⓑ ⓒ ⓓ
2.	ⓐ ⓑ ⓒ ⓓ	6.	ⓐ ⓑ ⓒ ⓓ	10.	ⓐ ⓑ ⓒ ⓓ	14.	ⓐ ⓑ ⓒ ⓓ	18.	ⓐ ⓑ ⓒ ⓓ	22.	ⓐ ⓑ ⓒ ⓓ
3.	ⓐ ⓑ ⓒ ⓓ	7.	ⓐ ⓑ ⓒ ⓓ	11.	ⓐ ⓑ ⓒ ⓓ	15.	ⓐ ⓑ ⓒ ⓓ	19.	ⓐ ⓑ ⓒ ⓓ	23.	ⓐ ⓑ ⓒ ⓓ
4.	ⓐ ⓑ ⓒ ⓓ	8.	ⓐ ⓑ ⓒ ⓓ	12.	ⓐ ⓑ ⓒ ⓓ	16.	ⓐ ⓑ ⓒ ⓓ	20.	ⓐ ⓑ ⓒ ⓓ	24.	ⓐ ⓑ ⓒ ⓓ

10

Food

1. **Among the given nutrients, milk is considered as a good source of ....**
(a) calcium (b) Vitamin B (c) carbohydrate (d) Vitamin C

2. **............ is considered a complete protein food.**
(a) Almond (b) Turmeric (c) Soybean (d) Amla

3. **The nutrient that is needed for a healthy immune system is ....**
(a) calcium (b) iodine (c) Vitamin K (d) Vitamin C

4. **Pulses are a good source of ....**
(a) carbohydrates (b) proteins
(c) fats (d) vitamins

5. **Which of the following is not considered as junk food?**
(a) Burger (b) Pizza (c) Oats (d) Noodles

6. **Identify the food item which is made from milk.**
(a) Fish (b) Potato (c) Cheese (d) Egg

7. **The food that comes from the leaves of a plant is ....**
(a) Spinach (b) Mango (c) Potato (d) Rice

8. **............... can be eaten only after cooking it properly.**
(a) Cucumber (b) Rice (c) Radish (d) Apple

9. **What kind of food does vegetarians eat?**
(a) Vegetables (b) Eggs (c) Meat (d) Fish

10. **Which of these foods is/are obtained from animals?**
(a) Egg (b) Milk (c) Meat (d) All of these

11. **Which of the following minerals help us to build strong bones and teeth?**
(a) Iodine (b) Calcium (c) Iron (d) Sodium

12. Which of the following food components does not provide any nutrients?

(a) Milk (b) Water (c) Fruit juice (d) Vegetable soup

13. Identify the food components that are rich in fat.

(a) Rice and maize (b) Milk, egg and beans

(c) Butter, cheese and oil (d) None of these

14. Guava, Lemon, Orange and Tomato are rich in ....

(a) Vitamin A (b) Vitamin B (c) Vitamin C (d) Vitamin D

15. Which of these can be eaten raw even without cooking?

(a) Brinjal (b) Potato (c) Pumpkin (d) Carrot

16. The diet that has the right amount of all the nutrients that our body needs is called ....

(a) healthy food (b) balanced diet (c) fast food (d) fantastic diet

17. What kind of food help us in keeping our muscles strong?

(a) Banana (b) Eggs (c) Soup (d) Pasta

18. People who eat fish, eggs and meat are called ....

(a) non-vegetarians (b) vegans

(c) vegetarians (d) None of these

19. Which food item is good for our health?

(a) Milk (b) Cold drink (c) Pizza (d) Burger

20. Consider the following statements and find true and false (T/F).

A. We should eat only meat to remain healthy.

B. Eating vegetables makes us ill.

Codes

	A	B		A	B
(a)	T	F	(b)	F	F
(c)	T	T	(d)	F	T

Darken your choice with HB Pencil

1.	ⓐ ⓑ ⓒ ⓓ	5.	ⓐ ⓑ ⓒ ⓓ	9.	ⓐ ⓑ ⓒ ⓓ	13.	ⓐ ⓑ ⓒ ⓓ	17.	ⓐ ⓑ ⓒ ⓓ
2.	ⓐ ⓑ ⓒ ⓓ	6.	ⓐ ⓑ ⓒ ⓓ	10.	ⓐ ⓑ ⓒ ⓓ	14.	ⓐ ⓑ ⓒ ⓓ	18.	ⓐ ⓑ ⓒ ⓓ
3.	ⓐ ⓑ ⓒ ⓓ	7.	ⓐ ⓑ ⓒ ⓓ	11.	ⓐ ⓑ ⓒ ⓓ	15.	ⓐ ⓑ ⓒ ⓓ	19.	ⓐ ⓑ ⓒ ⓓ
4.	ⓐ ⓑ ⓒ ⓓ	8.	ⓐ ⓑ ⓒ ⓓ	12.	ⓐ ⓑ ⓒ ⓓ	16.	ⓐ ⓑ ⓒ ⓓ	20.	ⓐ ⓑ ⓒ ⓓ

11

Plants

1. **Which one of the following is a tree?**

   (a) Neem (b) Money plant (c) Grapevine (d) Tulsi

2. **The leaves of .... are used as food.**

   (a) onion (b) cabbage (c) potato (d) ginger

3. **Fruits develop from ....**

   (a) leaves (b) flowers
   (c) seeds (d) stem

4. **Name the part of plant that develops inside the soil.**

   (a) Stem (b) Leaves
   (c) Root (d) Flowers

5. **Which among the following is not a plant?**

   (a) Rose plant (b) Mushroom
   (c) Banana tree (d) Coconut tree

6. **The plants which does not produce fruits is ....**

   (a) Marigold (b) Banana tree
   (c) Mango tree (d) Coconut tree

7. **The plant that will you normally find in desert area are ....**

   (a) Pineapple (b) Rice plant
   (c) Cactus (d) Mango tree

8. **Identify the incorrect pair.**

   (a) Root — Carrot (b) Stem — Potato
   (c) Flower — Cauliflower (d) Fruit — Cabbage

9. **Which one of the following is not a plant product?**

   (a) Flower (b) Fruit (c) Rubber (d) Butter

10. **The leaves of which plant can be eaten to cure cold and cough?**
(a) Rose (b) Tulsi (c) Mustard (d) Apple

11. **Find the odd one out.**
(a) Apple (b) Jasmine (c) Orange (d) Banana

12. **............... is root of a plant.**
(a) Peas (b) Radish (c) Tomato (d) Spinach

13. **Spot the plant that grows in water.**
(a) Sunflower (b) Lotus (c) Jasmine (d) None of these

14. **Which one of the following is not an example of climber plant?**
(a) Pea (b) Grapevine (c) Bean (d) Spinach

15. **............ is/are obtained from plants.**
(a) Paper (b) Animals (c) Medicine (d) Both (a) and (c)

16. **.............. help plants to absorb water and minerals.**
(a) Leaves (b) Root (c) Leaf (d) Flower

17. **Find the odd one out.**
(a) Jasmine (b) Lotus (c) Rose (d) Cactus

18. **Which one of the following parts of plant provides support to upper part of plant?**
(a) Root (b) Stem (c) Leaves (d) Fruits

19. **We get mint from which part of plant?**
(a) Root (b) Stem (c) Leaves (d) Flower

20. **Mint, Tulsi, Coriander all are examples of ....**
(a) stem (b) herbs (c) shrubs (d) seeds

21. **Find the odd one out on the basis of their colour.**
(a) Rose – Green (b) Sunflower – Yellow
(c) Brinjal – Purple (d) Grass – Green

22. **Oil is not obtained from which of the following plants?**
(a) Sunflower plant (b) Mustard plant
(c) Banyan plant (d) Coconut plant

23. Fruits, flowers and vegetables grow on many plants, except ....

(a) Grass (b) Mango tree

(c) Rose plant (d) Pea plant

24. Identify the incorrect option.

(a) Tea — Made from dried tea leaves

(b) Coffee — Made from coffee beans

(c) Sugar — Made from the juice of sugarcane

(d) Clove — Made from bamboo

25. Which one of the following has a strong stem?

(a) Climbers (b) Creepers

(c) Herbs (d) Tree

26. Which one of the following is an aquatic plant?

(a) Mint (b) Pumpkin

(c) Rose (d) Water lily

27. Match the following.

List I (Plant)	**List II** (Identity)
A. Sugarcane	1. To make perfumes
B. Jasmine	2. To make medicine
C. Neem	3. To make furniture
D. Bamboos	4. To make sugar

Codes

	A	B	C	D		A	B	C	D
(a)	4	1	2	3	(b)	1	2	3	4
(c)	2	3	1	4	(d)	3	4	1	2

Darken your choice with HB Pencil

1. ⓐ ⓑ ⓒ ⓓ	6. ⓐ ⓑ ⓒ ⓓ	11. ⓐ ⓑ ⓒ ⓓ	16. ⓐ ⓑ ⓒ ⓓ	21. ⓐ ⓑ ⓒ ⓓ	26. ⓐ ⓑ ⓒ ⓓ
2. ⓐ ⓑ ⓒ ⓓ	7. ⓐ ⓑ ⓒ ⓓ	12. ⓐ ⓑ ⓒ ⓓ	17. ⓐ ⓑ ⓒ ⓓ	22. ⓐ ⓑ ⓒ ⓓ	27. ⓐ ⓑ ⓒ ⓓ
3. ⓐ ⓑ ⓒ ⓓ	8. ⓐ ⓑ ⓒ ⓓ	13. ⓐ ⓑ ⓒ ⓓ	18. ⓐ ⓑ ⓒ ⓓ	23. ⓐ ⓑ ⓒ ⓓ	
4. ⓐ ⓑ ⓒ ⓓ	9. ⓐ ⓑ ⓒ ⓓ	14. ⓐ ⓑ ⓒ ⓓ	19. ⓐ ⓑ ⓒ ⓓ	24. ⓐ ⓑ ⓒ ⓓ	
5. ⓐ ⓑ ⓒ ⓓ	10. ⓐ ⓑ ⓒ ⓓ	15. ⓐ ⓑ ⓒ ⓓ	20. ⓐ ⓑ ⓒ ⓓ	25. ⓐ ⓑ ⓒ ⓓ	

12

Animals

1. **Identify the pair of animals that live in water.**

(a) Sparrow and Fish (b) Fish and Crocodile
(c) Elephant and Snake (d) Monkey and Rabbit

2. **Which one of the following is not a bird?**

(a) Peacock (b) Owl (c) Sparrow (d) Butterfly

3. **We obtain honey from which of the following insects?**

(a) Wasp (b) Butterfly
(c) Honey Bee (d) Grasshopper

4. **You will find .... on tree and .... in water.**

(a) snake, rabbit (b) monkey, frog
(c) lion, tiger (d) rabbit, owl

5. **How can you identify giraffe in the jungle?**

(a) It has a long neck. (b) It has a big trunk.
(c) It runs very fast. (d) It lives in water.

6. **Which animal makes the growling sound?**

(a) Tiger (b) Bear (c) Lion (d) Buffalo

7. **Which of the following is not correctly matched?**

(a) Bear – Cave (b) Horse – Stable
(c) Fish – Stable (d) Dog – Kennel

8. **The baby of a horse is known as ....**

(a) kid (b) cub (c) calf (d) foal

9. **.............. can easily see in the night.**

(a) Owl (b) Crow (c) Parrot (d) Sparrow

10. Identify the animal which lives in place shown in the given picture.

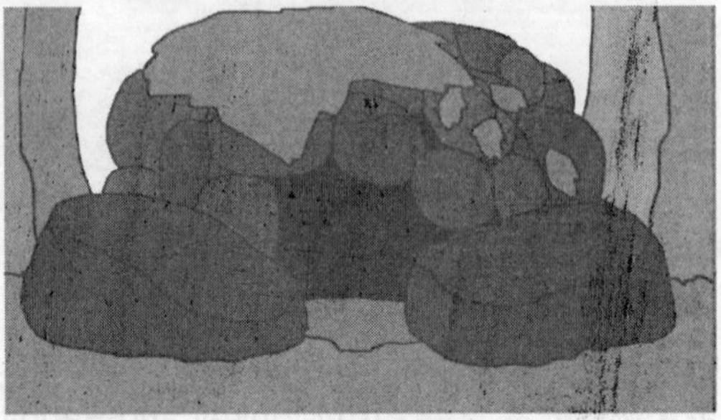

(a) Sheep (b) Lion
(c) Giraffe (d) Dog

11. Which of the following aquatic animals can live in water as well as on land?

(a) Fish (b) Dolphin
(c) Turtles (d) Whale

12. Identify the incorrect pair.

(a) Domestic animal – Cow (b) Wild animal – Elephant
(c) Water animal – Monkey (d) Pet animal – Dog

13. .... lives in the burrow.

(a) Sheep (b) Tiger
(c) Spider (d) Rabbit

14. Which of the following is kept in the cage shown below?

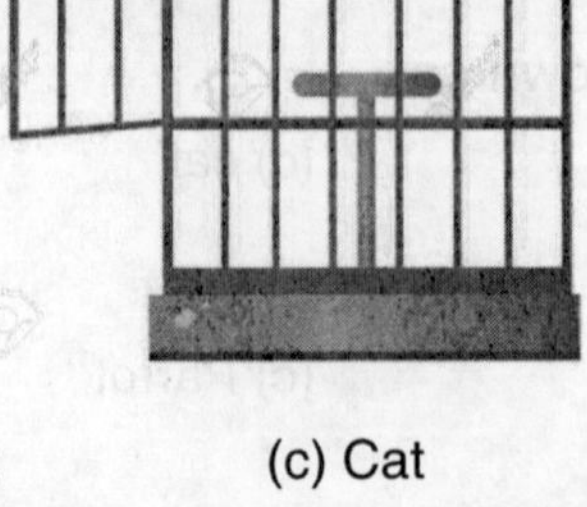

(a) Fish (b) Parrot (c) Cat (d) Dog

15. **The penguin and polar bear live in ....**

(a) desert (b) water
(c) ice region (d) mountains

16. **Which animal spins a web for making its own house?**

(a) Sparrow (b) Spider (c) Crab (d) Owl

17. **Which of the following is called the 'ship of the desert'?**

(a) Giraffe (b) Crow (c) Camel (d) Elephant

18. **Leather is made from the skin of which of the following animals?**

(a) Camel (b) Pigeon
(c) Ant (d) Fish

19. **Which animal makes the sound 'Neigh-Neigh'?**

(a) Donkey (b) Horse (c) Tiger (d) Cow

20. **The kitten is the baby of which of the following animals?**

(a) Cat (b) Pig (c) Snake (d) Cow

21. **Which of the following sounds is made by donkey?**

(a) Bark (b) Roar
(c) Moo (d) Bray

22. **Select the option that correctly fill the blank.**

Wild Animal: Wolf : : Water Animal : ....

(a) Octopus (b) Wolf (c) Spider (d) Pigeon

23. **Match the following.**

List I (Animals)	**List II** (Used For)
A. Hen	1. Milk
B. Buffalo	2. Carry heavy load
C. Donkey	3. Wool
D. Sheep	4. Eggs

Codes

	A	B	C	D		A	B	C	D
(a)	4	1	2	3	(b)	1	2	3	4
(c)	3	2	1	4	(d)	2	4	3	1

24. Match the animals with their food.

List I (Animals)	List II (Foods)
A. Tiger	1. Sugarcane
B. Elephant	2. Grass
C. Rabbit	3. Flesh
D. Goat	4. Carrot

Codes

	A	B	C	D		A	B	C	D
(a)	1	2	3	4	(b)	4	3	2	1
(c)	3	1	4	2	(d)	2	1	4	3

25. Match the following animals with their sound.

List I (Animals)	List II (Make Sound)
A. Cat	1. Caw
B. Lion	2. Baa
C. Sheep	3. Meow
D. Crow	4. Roar

Codes

	A	B	C	D		A	B	C	D
(a)	3	4	2	1	(b)	4	2	1	3
(c)	2	3	4	1	(d)	1	2	3	4

Darken your choice with HB Pencil

1.	ⓐ ⓑ ⓒ ⓓ	6.	ⓐ ⓑ ⓒ ⓓ	11.	ⓐ ⓑ ⓒ ⓓ	16.	ⓐ ⓑ ⓒ ⓓ	21.	ⓐ ⓑ ⓒ ⓓ
2.	ⓐ ⓑ ⓒ ⓓ	7.	ⓐ ⓑ ⓒ ⓓ	12.	ⓐ ⓑ ⓒ ⓓ	17.	ⓐ ⓑ ⓒ ⓓ	22.	ⓐ ⓑ ⓒ ⓓ
3.	ⓐ ⓑ ⓒ ⓓ	8.	ⓐ ⓑ ⓒ ⓓ	13.	ⓐ ⓑ ⓒ ⓓ	18.	ⓐ ⓑ ⓒ ⓓ	23.	ⓐ ⓑ ⓒ ⓓ
4.	ⓐ ⓑ ⓒ ⓓ	9.	ⓐ ⓑ ⓒ ⓓ	14.	ⓐ ⓑ ⓒ ⓓ	19.	ⓐ ⓑ ⓒ ⓓ	24.	ⓐ ⓑ ⓒ ⓓ
5.	ⓐ ⓑ ⓒ ⓓ	10.	ⓐ ⓑ ⓒ ⓓ	15.	ⓐ ⓑ ⓒ ⓓ	20.	ⓐ ⓑ ⓒ ⓓ	25.	ⓐ ⓑ ⓒ ⓓ

13

Computers

1. **The famous scientist Charles Babbage is also known as........... .**

   (a) Father of Television (b) Father of Books
   (c) Father of Computer (d) Father of Internet

2. **Which one of the following is an output device?**

   (a) Mouse (b) Keyboard (c) Monitor (d) Scanner

3. **What does 'P' stands for, in the terms of CPU?**

   (a) Power (b) Position (c) Playback (d) Processing

4. **The computer we use in our homes is also known as ....**

   (a) Mini computer (b) Personal computer
   (c) Private computer (d) Business computer

5. **Which of these is not a part of computer?**

   (a) 

   (b) 

   (c) 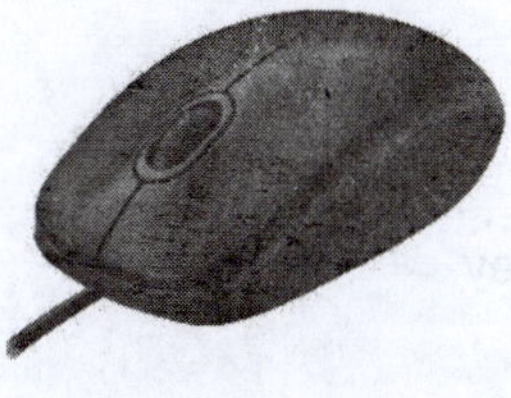

   (d) 

6. **By using which of the following will you give input to computer?**

   (a) Keyboard (b) Printer
   (c) Monitor (d) Speaker

7. You can store your data in which of the following devices?

(a) Pen drive (b) Mouse
(c) Monitor (d) Both (a) and (b)

8. Choose the places where computer is used?

(a) Banks (b) Airport
(c) Railway Station (d) All of these

9. Which one of the following is an audio device?

(a) Monitor (b) Speakers (c) Mouse (d) CPU

10. Identify the activity that can be performed by using the given device.

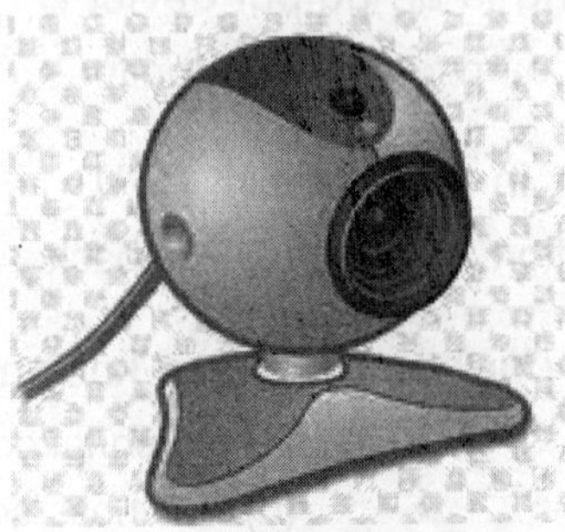

(a) Record video (b) Record voice
(c) Listen to music (d) Play games

11. .... is associated with left click, right click and scrolling.

(a) Mouse (b) Keyboard
(c) Printer (d) Joystick

12. The activitiy which you cannot do without Internet is ....

(a) listening music (b) playing games
(c) searching on google (d) painting

13. Which one of the following keys is the biggest key in keyboard?

(a) Caps lock key (b) Shift key
(c) Space key (d) Backspace key

14. Find the odd one out from the given options.

(a) Google (b) Yahoo (c) Facebook (d) Recycle Bin

15. The part of computer shown in the image is used for which purpose?

(a) Listening to music (b) Watching movies
(c) Storing data (d) Typing

16. Name the activities which can be done by using Internet.

(a) Bill payment (b) Watching online movies
(c) Video call (d) All of these

17. Which one of the following is not a basic device of computer?

(a) Headphones (b) Mouse (c) Keyboard (d) Monitor

18. Computers are used in ....

(a) banks (b) kitchen (c) forests (d) toilets

19. Where will you find the icons in the computer?

(a) On Keyboard (b) On Printer (c) On Screen (d) On CPU

20. What type of computer can be carried from one place to another?

(a) Personal computer (b) Laptop
(c) Super computer (d) Sonic computer

21. What is the right way to close the computer?

(a) Close the switch (b) Remove the wires
(c) By shutdown key (d) By restart key

Darken your choice with HB Pencil

1. ⓐ ⓑ ⓒ ⓓ	**5.** ⓐ ⓑ ⓒ ⓓ	**9.** ⓐ ⓑ ⓒ ⓓ	**13.** ⓐ ⓑ ⓒ ⓓ	**17.** ⓐ ⓑ ⓒ ⓓ	**21.** ⓐ ⓑ ⓒ ⓓ
2. ⓐ ⓑ ⓒ ⓓ	**6.** ⓐ ⓑ ⓒ ⓓ	**10.** ⓐ ⓑ ⓒ ⓓ	**14.** ⓐ ⓑ ⓒ ⓓ	**18.** ⓐ ⓑ ⓒ ⓓ	
3. ⓐ ⓑ ⓒ ⓓ	**7.** ⓐ ⓑ ⓒ ⓓ	**11.** ⓐ ⓑ ⓒ ⓓ	**15.** ⓐ ⓑ ⓒ ⓓ	**19.** ⓐ ⓑ ⓒ ⓓ	
4. ⓐ ⓑ ⓒ ⓓ	**8.** ⓐ ⓑ ⓒ ⓓ	**12.** ⓐ ⓑ ⓒ ⓓ	**16.** ⓐ ⓑ ⓒ ⓓ	**20.** ⓐ ⓑ ⓒ ⓓ	

14

Books and Authors

1. **Which of the following books is written by JK Rowling?**

(a) The Jungle Book (b) Harry Potter
(c) Ananda Math (d) Broken Wings

2. **The book, 'Playing it My Way' is written by.......... .**

(a) Sachin Tendulkar (b) Sourav Ganguly
(c) Virat Kohli (d) Rohit Sharma

3. **The book 'Discovery of India' is written by.......... .**

(a) Mahatma Gandhi (b) Sardar Patel
(c) Jawaharlal Nehru (d) None of these

4. **Which one of the following books is written by Narendra Modi?**

(a) Panchtantra (b) Kesari
(c) Exam Warriors (d) Godan

5. **Which of the following is the writer of the book 'The Jungle Book'?**

(a) Sarojini Naidu (b) JK Rowling
(c) Rudyard Kipling (d) Kautilya

6. **Which of the following books is written by Bankim Chandra Chatterjee?**

(a) Discovery of India (b) My Experiment with Truth
(c) Ananda Math (d) Panchtantra

7. **The famous book 'Two States' is written by ....**

(a) Kiran Bedi (b) Chetan Bhagat
(c) Shashi Tharoor (d) Mahatma Gandhi

8. **Which one of the following books is an autobiography of Mahatma Gandhi?**

(a) Discovery of India (b) Runs in Ruins
(c) Bunch of Old Letters (d) My Experiment with Truth

9. **Who had written the epic 'Ramayana'?**
(a) Rishi Valmiki (b) Ved Vyasa
(c) Rishi Vashistha (d) Parashurama

10. **Which one of the following books is written by our former President APJ Abdul Kalam?**
(a) The Broken Wings (b) Wings of Water
(c) Wings of Fire (d) Conquest to Self

11. **Which one of the following epics was written by Ved Vyasa?**
(a) Mahabharata (b) Ramayana
(c) Vishnu Puran (d) Godan

12. **Who is the writer of the famous novel 'Hamlet'?**
(a) Christina Lamb (b) Enid Blyton
(c) William Shakespeare (d) Chetan Bhagat

13. **Which one of the famous books is written by the author Jonathan Swift?**
(a) Winnie-the-Pooh (b) The Snow White
(c) Cinderella (d) Gulliver's Travels

14. **Which one of the following is the writer of the book 'Panchtantra'?**
(a) Jawaharlal Nehru (b) Sardar Patel
(c) Chetan Bhagat (d) Vishnu Sharma

15. **The 'Ramcharitmanas' is written by ....**
(a) Surdas (b) Tulsidas
(c) Ramdas (d) Ved Vyasa

16. **The book, 'Winnie-the-Pooh' was written by ....**
(a) Rudyard Kipling (b) Roald Dahl
(c) JK Rowling (d) AA Milne

Darken your choice with HB Pencil

1.	ⓐ ⓑ ⓒ ⓓ	4.	ⓐ ⓑ ⓒ ⓓ	7.	ⓐ ⓑ ⓒ ⓓ	10.	ⓐ ⓑ ⓒ ⓓ	13.	ⓐ ⓑ ⓒ ⓓ	16.	ⓐ ⓑ ⓒ ⓓ
2.	ⓐ ⓑ ⓒ ⓓ	5.	ⓐ ⓑ ⓒ ⓓ	8.	ⓐ ⓑ ⓒ ⓓ	11.	ⓐ ⓑ ⓒ ⓓ	14.	ⓐ ⓑ ⓒ ⓓ		
3.	ⓐ ⓑ ⓒ ⓓ	6.	ⓐ ⓑ ⓒ ⓓ	9.	ⓐ ⓑ ⓒ ⓓ	12.	ⓐ ⓑ ⓒ ⓓ	15.	ⓐ ⓑ ⓒ ⓓ		

15

Sports

1. **What is the national game of our country?**
   (a) Cricket
   (b) Hockey
   (c) Kabaddi
   (d) Football

2. **Which one of the following is not an indoor game?**
   (a) Carrom
   (b) Ludo
   (c) Chess
   (d) Cricket

3. **The given image depicts which of the following sports?**

   (a) Basketball
   (b) Cricket
   (c) Football
   (d) Volleyball

4. **The equipments like- helmet, bat, gloves are used in which sports?**
   (a) Basketball
   (b) Cricket
   (c) Football
   (d) Volleyball

5. **Which of the following sports use a net?**
   (a) Lawn Tennis
   (b) Volleyball
   (c) Badminton
   (d) All of these

6. **Which of the following sports is played without ball?**
   (a) Badminton
   (b) Basketball
   (c) Volleyball
   (d) Hockey

7. **Identify the sports personality shown in the picture.**

(a) Dhyan Chand
(b) Sardara Singh
(c) Baichung Bhutia
(d) Harbhajan Singh

8. **Which one of the following sports is played by the help of air guns?**

(a) Shooting
(b) Swimming
(c) Polo
(d) Hockey

9. **The picture of the sticks shown below belongs to which sports?**

(a) Cricket
(b) Hockey
(c) Football
(d) Volleyball

10. **Identify the sports personality shown in the picture.**

(a) Mithali Raj
(b) Sania Mirza
(c) Mary Kom
(d) Saina Nehwal

11. **The given court represent which of the following sports?**

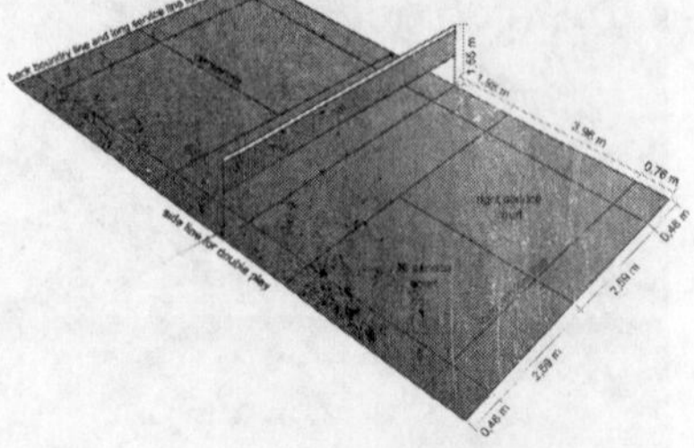

(a) Hockey
(b) Football
(c) Badminton
(d) Swimming

12. **If 'UMPIRE' is related to 'Cricket', then 'REFEREE' is related to......... .**

(a) Chess
(b) Football
(c) Ludo
(d) Hide and Seek

13. **Identify the sport shown in the picture given below.**

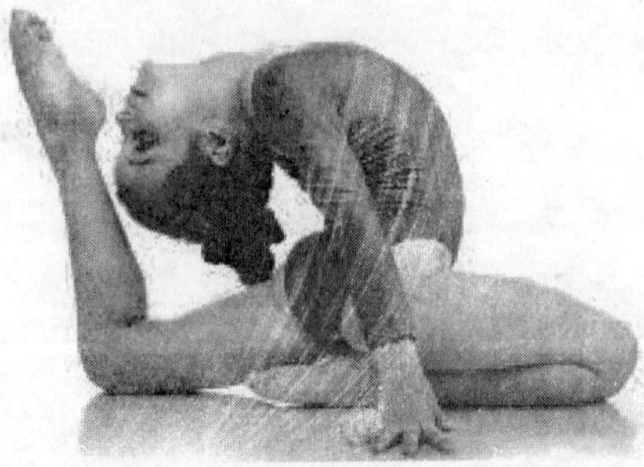

(a) Gymnastics
(b) Judo
(c) Tennis
(d) Basketball

14. **How many kings are there in a game of chess?**

(a) 2 (b) 3 (c) 1 (d) 4

15. **Which one of the following sportspersons is not related to cricket?**

(a) Sachin Tendulkar
(b) Virat Kohli
(c) Abhinav Bindra
(d) Rohit Sharma

16. **Saina Nehwal is related to which sports?**

(a) Cricket
(b) Hockey
(c) Boxing
(d) Badminton

17. Sunil Chhetri is related to which sport?

(a) Football (b) Hockey
(c) Cricket (d) Badminton

18. Identify the sportsperson shown in the image.

(a) MS Dhoni (b) Yuvraj Singh
(c) Virat Kohli (d) Rohit Sharma

Darken your choice with HB Pencil

1. ⓐ ⓑ ⓒ ⓓ	4. ⓐ ⓑ ⓒ ⓓ	7. ⓐ ⓑ ⓒ ⓓ	10. ⓐ ⓑ ⓒ ⓓ	13. ⓐ ⓑ ⓒ ⓓ	16. ⓐ ⓑ ⓒ ⓓ
2. ⓐ ⓑ ⓒ ⓓ	5. ⓐ ⓑ ⓒ ⓓ	8. ⓐ ⓑ ⓒ ⓓ	11. ⓐ ⓑ ⓒ ⓓ	14. ⓐ ⓑ ⓒ ⓓ	17. ⓐ ⓑ ⓒ ⓓ
3. ⓐ ⓑ ⓒ ⓓ	6. ⓐ ⓑ ⓒ ⓓ	9. ⓐ ⓑ ⓒ ⓓ	12. ⓐ ⓑ ⓒ ⓓ	15. ⓐ ⓑ ⓒ ⓓ	18. ⓐ ⓑ ⓒ ⓓ

16

Important Days and Dates

1. **World Health Day is celebrated on which date?**
   (a) 14th February (b) 7th April
   (c) 1st January (d) 31st December

2. **Independence Day is celebrated in India on which date?**
   (a) 31st December (b) 15th August
   (c) 26th January (d) 2nd October

3. **Every year 26th January is celebrated as ....**
   (a) Republic Day (b) Independence Day
   (c) Gandhi Jayanti (d) Christmas Day

4. **Which day is celebrated to give tribute to Father of the Nation?**
   (a) Children's Day (b) Gandhi Jayanti
   (c) Republic Day (d) Independence Day

5. **National Unity Day is celebrated on which date?**
   (a) 2nd October (b) 31st October
   (c) 1st January (d) 31st December

6. **On which of the following dates, the Earth Day is celebrated ?**
   (a) 18th April (b) 23rd April
   (c) 31st April (d) 22nd April

7. **.............. is celebrated on 5th June every year for the protection of the environment.**
   (a) World Heritage Day (b) English Language Day
   (c) World Environment Day (d) World Science Day

8. **2nd October is celebrated as the .... all around the world.**

   (a) International Day of Non-Violence (b) Father's Day
   (c) Republic Day (d) Independence Day

9. **Which day is celebrated every year on 14th November?**

   (a) Teacher's Day (b) Children's Day
   (c) Mother's Day (d) Father's Day

10. **5th September is celebrated in India as ....**

    (a) Doctor's Day (b) Air Force Day
    (c) Teacher's Day (d) Mother's Day

11. **When is World Earth Day celebrated?**

    (a) 22nd April (b) 14th November
    (c) 5th September (d) 15th August

12. **Students along with teachers are planting trees in the school ground. According to you, which day are they celebrating?**

    (a) World Environment Day (b) English Language Day
    (c) World Science Day (d) World Water Day

Darken your choice with HB Pencil

1.	ⓐ ⓑ ⓒ ⓓ	3.	ⓐ ⓑ ⓒ ⓓ	5.	ⓐ ⓑ ⓒ ⓓ	7.	ⓐ ⓑ ⓒ ⓓ	9.	ⓐ ⓑ ⓒ ⓓ	11.	ⓐ ⓑ ⓒ ⓓ
2.	ⓐ ⓑ ⓒ ⓓ	4.	ⓐ ⓑ ⓒ ⓓ	6.	ⓐ ⓑ ⓒ ⓓ	8.	ⓐ ⓑ ⓒ ⓓ	10.	ⓐ ⓑ ⓒ ⓓ	12.	ⓐ ⓑ ⓒ ⓓ

Practice Set 01

Time : 60 Mins. Max. Marks : 35

General Instructions

1. This question paper contains 35 questions.
2. Each question carries 1 mark.
3. All questions are compulsory. There is no negative marking.
4. Use HB pencil / Blue ball point pen to mark your choice of answer by darkening the circles on the OMR Sheet.

1. If we fall ill, who gives us medicines, so that we can become healthy?

(a) Doctor (b) Engineer
(c) Policeman (d) Postman

2. Which one of the following planets is the biggest planet in our Solar System?

(a) Mars (b) Saturn (c) Jupiter (d) Earth

3. The capital of Maharashtra is ....

(a) Patna (b) Delhi (c) Kanpur (d) Mumbai

4. Which one of the following personalities has never been the Prime Minister of India?

(a) APJ Abdul Kalam (b) Atal Bihari Vajpayee
(c) Manmohan Singh (d) Jawaharlal Nehru

5. The tools shown in the image are used by which of the following?

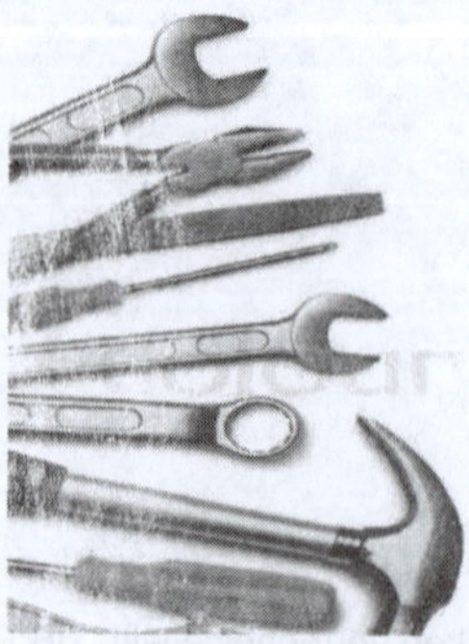

(a) Plumber (b) Mechanic
(c) Doctor (d) Musician

6. **The 'Guru Granth Sahib' is the holy book of which of the following religions?**

(a) Hindus (b) Sikhs (c) Muslims (d) Christians

7. **Gateway of India is located in ....**

(a) Delhi (b) Kolkata (c) Chennai (d) Mumbai

8. **Which one of the following instruments is associated with Goddess Saraswati?**

(a) Guitar (b) Violin
(c) Veena (d) Tabla

9. **We need .... to taste different things.**

(a) hand (b) eyes (c) tongue (d) ears

10. **Which one of the following organs is considerd as internal organ of our body?**

(a) Tongue (b) Nails (c) Chest (d) Liver

11. **The food items that are made from milk ....**

(a) Fish (b) Potato (c) Curd (d) Egg

12. **The baby of which of the following animals is known as kid?**

(a) Rabbit (b) Horse (c) Donkey (d) Goat

13. **The things which are provided by plants is/are ....**

(a) cereals (b) coffee
(c) vegetables (d) All of these

14. **Which of the following activities can we perform on our computer?**

(a) Watching movies (b) Painting
(c) Searching on Internet (d) All of these

15. **Pulses are a good source of ....**

(a) carbohydrates (b) proteins
(c) fats (d) vitamins

16. **Gandhi Jayanti is celebrated every year on which of the following dates?**

(a) 1st October (b) 31st December
(c) 2nd October (d) 1st January

17. **Which of the following sports uses a bigger ball than the others?**

(a) Cricket (b) Golf (c) Football (d) Hockey

18. **Identify the famous sportsperson shown in the given picture.**

(a) Sania Mirza (b) Saina Nehwal
(c) Mary Kom (d) Mithali Raj

19. **Our planet Earth is also known as....... .**
(a) Red planet (b) Pink planet
(c) Green planet (d) Blue planet

20. **How many Union Territories are there in India?**
(a) 9 (b) 8 (c) 7 (d) 10

21. **The first woman President of our country is ....**
(a) Indira Gandhi (b) Sarojini Naidu
(c) Pratibha Patil (d) Annie Besant

22. **The given flag is associated with which of the following countries?**

(a) Australia (b) Brazil (c) China (d) New Zealand

23. **Goddess Durga is worshipped in which festival?**
(a) Holi (b) Navratri
(c) Bihu (d) Ganesh Chaturthi

24. **Kathak is a famous dance form of which state?**
(a) Uttar Pradesh (b) Gujarat
(c) Rajasthan (d) Maharashtra

25. **Identify the instrument shown in the picture given below.**

(a) Veena (b) Sitar (c) Guitar (d) Piano

26. **............... also is known as 'Science City of India'.**

(a) Hyderabad (b) Chennai (c) Bengaluru (d) Shimla

27. **Which organ pumps blood in our whole body?**

(a) Brain (b) Heart
(c) Kidneys (d) Stomach

28. **Name the animal that does not eat flesh.**

(a) Lion (b) Bear (c) Tiger (d) Cow

29. **............ leaves can be eaten to cure cold and cough.**

(a) Rose (b) Tulsi (c) Lotus (d) Mustard

30. **Enter, space and caps lock keys are found in which one of them?**

(a) Monitor (b) Mouse (c) Keyboard (d) CPU

31. **Identify the personality shown in the given picture.**

(a) Narendra Modi (b) Ram Nath Kovind
(c) Yogi Adityanath (d) Amit Shah

32. **Which one of the following days is celebrated on 22nd April every year?**

(a) Water Day (b) Earth Day

(c) Independence Day (d) Non-Violence Day

33. **Which one of the following sports is associated with the personality Mary Kom?**

(a) Swimming (b) Archery (c) Boxing (d) Wrestling

34. **We will not be able to listen anything, if we do not have ....**

(a) eyes (b) ears (c) nose (d) skin

35. **Match the following.**

List I (Food)	List II (Source)
A. Orange	1. Hen
B. Sugar	2. Cow
C. Milk	3. Sugarcane
D. Eggs	4. Plant

Codes

	A	B	C	D		A	B	C	D
(a)	1	3	2	4	(b)	4	3	2	1
(c)	2	3	4	1	(d)	1	2	3	4

Darken your choice with HB Pencil

1.	a	b	c	d	7.	a	b	c	d	13.	a	b	c	d	19.	a	b	c	d	25.	a	b	c	d	31.	a	b	c	d
2.	a	b	c	d	8.	a	b	c	d	14.	a	b	c	d	20.	a	b	c	d	26.	a	b	c	d	32.	a	b	c	d
3.	a	b	c	d	9.	a	b	c	d	15.	a	b	c	d	21.	a	b	c	d	27.	a	b	c	d	33.	a	b	c	d
4.	a	b	c	d	10.	a	b	c	d	16.	a	b	c	d	22.	a	b	c	d	28.	a	b	c	d	34.	a	b	c	d
5.	a	b	c	d	11.	a	b	c	d	17.	a	b	c	d	23.	a	b	c	d	29.	a	b	c	d	35.	a	b	c	d
6.	a	b	c	d	12.	a	b	c	d	18.	a	b	c	d	24.	a	b	c	d	30.	a	b	c	d					

Practice Set 02

Time : 60 Mins. Max. Marks : 35

General Instructions

1. This question paper contains 35 questions.
2. Each question carries 1 mark.
3. All questions are compulsory. There is no negative marking.
4. Use HB pencil / Blue ball point pen to mark your choice of answer by darkening the circles on the OMR Sheet.

1. Which one of the following players is associated with football?

(a) Jasprit Bumrah (b) Virat Kohli

(c) Dinesh Patel (d) Sunil Chhetri

2. Identify the output device from the pictures given below.

(a) 

(b) 

(c) 

(d) 

3. Which one of the following is an aquatic plant?

(a) Mint (b) Pumpkin

(c) Rose (d) Water lily

4. On which of the following dates Teacher's Day is celebrated every year?

(a) 5th January (b) 5th April

(c) 5th December (d) 5th September

5. Identify the former Prime Minister of India shown in the image.

(a) Kiran Bedi (b) Pratibha Patil
(c) Indira Gandhi (d) Sarojini Naidu

6. Which of the following plants is/are used to make medicines?
(a) Neem (b) Tulsi
(c) Mint (d) All of these

7. Which of the following types of animal live in jungle?
(a) Pet animals (b) Domestic animals
(c) Water animals (d) Wild animals

8. Pulses are a good source of ....
(a) carbohydrates (b) proteins
(c) fats (d) vitamins

9. Which one of the following organs is responsible for decision-making, thinking and learning?
(a) Heart (b) Hairs
(c) Stomach (d) Brain

10. The tallest building 'Burj Khalifa' is located in which of the following countries?
(a) United States of America (b) United Kingdom
(c) Russia (d) United Arab Emirates

11. We can see a beautiful rainbow in the sky with the help of which organ?
(a) Nose (b) Eyes
(c) Ears (d) Lips

12. In which of the following religions, people worship Lord Jesus?
(a) Muslim (b) Jainism
(c) Christian (d) Sikh

13. **Identify the country from the given flag.**

(a) USA (b) Russia (c) China (d) Pakistan

14. **Identify the dance form shown in the picture given below.**

(a) Bhangra (b) Bharatanatyam (c) Kathakali (d) Manipuri

15. **The animal which lives in a burrow is ....**

(a) sheep (b) tiger (c) spider (d) rabbit

16. **Mars is also known as ....**

(a) Blue planet (b) Red planet (c) Green planet (d) White planet

17. **In which of the following places will you go to study and learn new things?**

(a) Restaurant (b) School (c) Park (d) Market

18. **Which of the following sports is being played by a ball and a racket?**

(a) Badminton (b) Cricket
(c) Hockey (d) Tennis

19. **What does 'C' stands for in the full form of CPU?**

(a) Control (b) Collect (c) Central (d) Common

20. **............ is celebrated on 5th June every year for the protection of our surroundings.**

(a) World Heritage Day (b) English Language Day
(c) World Environment Day (d) World Science Day

21. **The book 'Exam Warrior' is written by which of the following personalities?**

(a) Jawaharlal Nehru (b) Indira Gandhi
(c) APJ Abdul Kalam (d) Narendra Modi

22. **Which one of the following does not come under the category of a tree?**

(a) Rose (b) Coconut (c) Banyan (d) Mango

23. **The part of plant that provides support to upper parts of the plant is ....**

(a) root (b) stem
(c) leaves (d) flowers

24. **Which of the following animals makes a sound 'Croak'?**

(a) Pig (b) Cow (c) Frog (d) Dog

25. **............... can be eaten raw, without cooking.**

(a) Brinjal (b) Potato (c) Pumpkin (d) Mango

26. **What is located in the upper part of the body?**

(a) Shoulder (b) Foot (c) Toe (d) Knee

27. **The city of Hyderabad is famous for which of the following monuments?**

(a) Qutub Minar (b) Taj Mahal
(c) Sanchi Stupa (d) Char Minar

28. **Which one of the following is not the notes of Sur in Hindustani music?**

(a) Sa (b) Re (c) Ga (d) Ri

29. **The festival which is celebrated by our Muslim friends at the end of the fasting month of Ramadan is ....**

(a) Eid ul-Fitr (b) Holi (c) Onam (d) Navratri

30. **The city 'Canberra' is the capital of which of the following countries?**

(a) China (b) Japan (c) Brazil (d) Australia

31. The famous leader Sarvepalli Radhakrishnan was the first .... of India.

(a) Prime Minister (b) Home Minister (c) President (d) Vice-President

32. What does 'P' stands for in 'CPU'?

(a) Power (b) Position (c) Playback (d) Processing

33. What is the position of the planet Earth from the Sun?

(a) Second (b) Fourth (c) Sixth (d) Third

34. Which one of the following makes wooden tables and chairs for our homes?

(a) Mechanic (b) Painter (c) Carpenter (d) Electrician

35. Identify the famous sportsperson shown in the given picture.

(a) Virat Kohli (b) Hardik Pandya

(c) Rohit Sharma (d) Harbhajan Singh

Darken your choice with HB Pencil

1.	ⓐ ⓑ ⓒ ⓓ	**7.**	ⓐ ⓑ ⓒ ⓓ	**13.**	ⓐ ⓑ ⓒ ⓓ	**19.**	ⓐ ⓑ ⓒ ⓓ	**25.**	ⓐ ⓑ ⓒ ⓓ	**31.**	ⓐ ⓑ ⓒ ⓓ
2.	ⓐ ⓑ ⓒ ⓓ	**8.**	ⓐ ⓑ ⓒ ⓓ	**14.**	ⓐ ⓑ ⓒ ⓓ	**20.**	ⓐ ⓑ ⓒ ⓓ	**26.**	ⓐ ⓑ ⓒ ⓓ	**32.**	ⓐ ⓑ ⓒ ⓓ
3.	ⓐ ⓑ ⓒ ⓓ	**9.**	ⓐ ⓑ ⓒ ⓓ	**15.**	ⓐ ⓑ ⓒ ⓓ	**21.**	ⓐ ⓑ ⓒ ⓓ	**27.**	ⓐ ⓑ ⓒ ⓓ	**33.**	ⓐ ⓑ ⓒ ⓓ
4.	ⓐ ⓑ ⓒ ⓓ	**10.**	ⓐ ⓑ ⓒ ⓓ	**16.**	ⓐ ⓑ ⓒ ⓓ	**22.**	ⓐ ⓑ ⓒ ⓓ	**28.**	ⓐ ⓑ ⓒ ⓓ	**34.**	ⓐ ⓑ ⓒ ⓓ
5.	ⓐ ⓑ ⓒ ⓓ	**11.**	ⓐ ⓑ ⓒ ⓓ	**17.**	ⓐ ⓑ ⓒ ⓓ	**23.**	ⓐ ⓑ ⓒ ⓓ	**29.**	ⓐ ⓑ ⓒ ⓓ	**35.**	ⓐ ⓑ ⓒ ⓓ
6.	ⓐ ⓑ ⓒ ⓓ	**12.**	ⓐ ⓑ ⓒ ⓓ	**18.**	ⓐ ⓑ ⓒ ⓓ	**24.**	ⓐ ⓑ ⓒ ⓓ	**30.**	ⓐ ⓑ ⓒ ⓓ		

Answer Sheet

Chapter 01

1. (c) 2. (d) 3. (c) 4. (c) 5. (a) 6. (a) 7. (b) 8. (b) 9. (b) 10. (a)
11. (d) 12. (d) 13. (c) 14. (a) 15. (d) 16. (a) 17. (d) 18. (c) 19. (c) 20. (b)
21. (d) 22. (c) 23. (a)

Chapter 02

1. (b) 2. (b) 3. (c) 4. (b) 5. (a) 6. (d) 7. (b) 8. (a) 9. (d) 10. (a)
11. (d) 12. (d) 13. (a) 14. (b) 15. (c) 16. (b) 17. (a) 18. (b) 19. (a) 20. (b)
21. (b) 22. (b) 23. (c) 24. (b)

Chapter 03

1. (b) 2. (b) 3. (d) 4. (b) 5. (c) 6. (b) 7. (c) 8. (d) 9. (a) 10. (b)
11. (d) 12. (c) 13. (c) 14. (a) 15. (a) 16. (d) 17. (b) 18. (c) 19. (a) 20. (d)
21. (a) 22. (d) 23. (c) 24. (d) 25. (c)

Chapter 04

1. (d) 2. (a) 3. (d) 4. (d) 5. (c) 6. (c) 7. (b) 8. (c) 9. (a) 10. (c)
11. (a) 12. (b) 13. (b) 14. (a) 15. (b) 16. (a) 17. (b) 18. (b)

Chapter 05

1. (a) 2. (b) 3. (d) 4. (a) 5. (b) 6. (b) 7. (c) 8. (b) 9. (c) 10. (b)
11. (a) 12. (d) 13. (c) 14. (a) 15. (c) 16. (a)

Chapter 06

1. (a) 2. (d) 3. (b) 4. (d) 5. (d) 6. (a) 7. (b) 8. (d) 9. (b) 10. (c)
11. (b) 12. (b) 13. (c) 14. (d) 15. (b) 16. (c) 17. (b) 18. (c) 19. (a) 20. (b)
21. (c) 22. (a) 23. (d) 24. (c) 25. (b) 26. (b) 27. (c) 28. (c)

Chapter 07

1. (b) 2. (d) 3. (a) 4. (c) 5. (a) 6. (d) 7. (d) 8. (a) 9. (b) 10. (d)
11. (d) 12. (a) 13. (b) 14. (c) 15. (a) 16. (b) 17. (b) 18. (c) 19. (a) 20. (d)
21. (a) 22. (d)

Chapter 08

1. (a)	**2.** (c)	**3.** (c)	**4.** (d)	**5.** (c)	**6.** (d)	**7.** (d)	**8.** (a)	**9.** (c)	**10.** (a)
11. (d)	**12.** (d)	**13.** (c)	**14.** (c)	**15.** (b)	**16.** (b)	**17.** (a)	**18.** (a)	**19.** (a)	**20.** (d)
21. (d)	**22.** (c)	**23.** (b)	**24.** (a)						

Chapter 09

1. (a)	**2.** (b)	**3.** (a)	**4.** (d)	**5.** (a)	**6.** (c)	**7.** (d)	**8.** (a)	**9.** (d)	**10.** (d)
11. (b)	**12.** (d)	**13.** (b)	**14.** (c)	**15.** (d)	**16.** (c)	**17.** (c)	**18.** (d)	**19.** (d)	**20.** (a)
21. (a)	**22.** (a)	**23.** (c)	**24.** (d)						

Chapter 10

1. (a)	**2.** (c)	**3.** (d)	**4.** (b)	**5.** (c)	**6.** (c)	**7.** (a)	**8.** (b)	**9.** (a)	**10.** (d)
11. (b)	**12.** (b)	**13.** (c)	**14.** (c)	**15.** (d)	**16.** (b)	**17.** (b)	**18.** (a)	**19.** (b)	**20.** (a)

Chapter 11

1. (a)	**2.** (b)	**3.** (b)	**4.** (c)	**5.** (b)	**6.** (a)	**7.** (c)	**8.** (d)	**9.** (d)	**10.** (b)
11. (b)	**12.** (b)	**13.** (b)	**14.** (b)	**15.** (d)	**16.** (b)	**17.** (d)	**18.** (b)	**19.** (c)	**20.** (b)
21. (a)	**22.** (c)	**23.** (a)	**24.** (d)	**25.** (d)	**26.** (d)	**27.** (a)			

Chapter 12

1. (b)	**2.** (d)	**3.** (c)	**4.** (b)	**5.** (a)	**6.** (b)	**7.** (c)	**8.** (d)	**9.** (a)	**10.** (b)
11. (c)	**12.** (c)	**13.** (d)	**14.** (b)	**15.** (c)	**16.** (b)	**17.** (c)	**18.** (a)	**19.** (b)	**20.** (a)
21. (d)	**22.** (a)	**23.** (a)	**24.** (c)	**25.** (a)					

Chapter 13

1. (c)	**2.** (c)	**3.** (d)	**4.** (b)	**5.** (a)	**6.** (a)	**7.** (a)	**8.** (d)	**9.** (b)	**10.** (a)
11. (a)	**12.** (c)	**13.** (c)	**14.** (d)	**15.** (c)	**16.** (d)	**17.** (a)	**18.** (a)	**19.** (c)	**20.** (b)
21. (c)									

Chapter 14

1. (b)	**2.** (a)	**3.** (c)	**4.** (c)	**5.** (c)	**6.** (c)	**7.** (b)	**8.** (d)	**9.** (a)	**10.** (c)
11. (a)	**12.** (c)	**13.** (d)	**14.** (d)	**15.** (b)	**16.** (d)				

Chapter 15

1. (b)	**2.** (d)	**3.** (a)	**4.** (b)	**5.** (d)	**6.** (a)	**7.** (b)	**8.** (a)	**9.** (b)	**10.** (c)
11. (c)	**12.** (b)	**13.** (a)	**14.** (a)	**15.** (c)	**16.** (d)	**17.** (a)	**18.** (b)		

Chapter 16

1. (b)	**2.** (b)	**3.** (a)	**4.** (b)	**5.** (b)	**6.** (d)	**7.** (c)	**8.** (a)	**9.** (b)	**10.** (c)
11. (a)	**12.** (a)								

Practice Set 01

1. (a)	**2.** (c)	**3.** (d)	**4.** (a)	**5.** (b)	**6.** (b)	**7.** (d)	**8.** (c)	**9.** (c)	**10.** (d)
11. (c)	**12.** (d)	**13.** (d)	**14.** (d)	**15.** (b)	**16.** (c)	**17.** (c)	**18.** (b)	**19.** (d)	**20.** (b)
21. (c)	**22.** (a)	**23.** (b)	**24.** (a)	**25.** (c)	**26.** (c)	**27.** (b)	**28.** (d)	**29.** (b)	**30.** (c)
31. (b)	**32.** (b)	**33.** (c)	**34.** (b)	**35.** (b)					

Practice Set 02

1. (d)	**2.** (c)	**3.** (d)	**4.** (d)	**5.** (c)	**6.** (d)	**7.** (d)	**8.** (b)	**9.** (d)	**10.** (d)
11. (b)	**12.** (c)	**13.** (c)	**14.** (c)	**15.** (d)	**16.** (b)	**17.** (b)	**18.** (d)	**19.** (c)	**20.** (c)
21. (d)	**22.** (a)	**23.** (b)	**24.** (c)	**25.** (d)	**26.** (a)	**27.** (d)	**28.** (d)	**29.** (a)	**30.** (d)
31. (d)	**32.** (d)	**33.** (d)	**34.** (c)	**35.** (c)					